Low Carb Filipino Recipe Book

Book

Easy Low Carb Filipino Favorites

TABLE OF CONTENTS

Cheese Quesadilla

Ingredients:

Wraps:

1/3 cup Mexican blend cheese (Kraft Shredded)

1 tbsp. sour cream

2 tbsp. salsa

1/2 pat butter (about 1 tsp)

Instructions:

Take 1 low carb wrap and lightly butter.

Place butter side down in frypan/griddle

Add cheese evenly, covering most of wrap (leave about 1/4 inch at edge).

Cover and watch for cheese to be mostly melted.

When most of cheese is melted, close the quesadilla by folding in half.

Cook until browned and crispy.

Flip over and cook other side until browned and crispy

Cut in 3 wedges and serve with sour cream and low sugar salsa.

Asian Chicken Salad

Ingredients:

3 Oz grilled Skinless, Boneless Chicken Breast, cubed

1 Cup dark salad greens (red lettuce, romaine and spinach greens)

1/4 cup Mandarin Orange sections, pits and membranes removed

3 Cherry Tomatoes

2 Tbsp. Sliced Almonds

1/4 Cup Matchstick Carrots

1/4 Cup Snow Peas

Instructions:

Toss all ingredients together and enjoy with your favorite low Cal Asian inspired dressing

Twice Baked Cauliflower

Ingredients:

1 large head cauliflower

4 oz. low fat cream cheese

1 tbsp. butter

1/2 cup fat free sour cream

1/4 cup minced green onions

1/4 cup freshly grated parmesan cheese

5 slices bacon, cooked very crisp and crumbled

1 cup reduced fat sharp cheddar cheese

Instructions:

Preheat oven to 350 F. Cut out stem and core from cauliflower, and cut into small pieces. Cook in large pot of boiling water until cauliflower is tender, but not overly soft. Drain well and mash with potato masher, leaving some chunks. Mix in cream cheese, butter (if using), sour cream, green onion, Parmesan, and 3/4 of the bacon.

Spread evenly in an 8 X 8 inch glass casserole dish. Sprinkle with cheddar cheese and reserved bacon. Bake 30-35 minutes, or until hot and bubbly.

Tuna Melt

Ingredients:

1 can albacore tuna packed in water

1 tbsp. pickle relish

2 tbsp. low fat mayonnaise

3 tbsp. chopped onion

2 slices medium tomato

1 slice Swiss cheese

1 English muffin

Instructions:

Preheat oven to 350 degrees

Mix tuna, onion, mayonnaise & pickle relish in a bowl until well combined.

Lightly toast English muffin place a spoonful of tuna mixture on each half of English muffin top with one slice of tomato and half piece Swiss cheese each.

Bake for about 10 minutes or until cheese is bubbly

CHICKEN PANCIT

Ingredients:

4 Chicken Breast (skin removed)

1 package Canton Noodles

1 cup Sliced Carrots

1 cup Sliced Celery

1 cup chopped Onions

1/2 medium size Cabbage

3 cloves of Garlic

3 tbsp. Extra Virgin Olive Oil

Pepper and Salt to taste

Instructions:

Boil the skinless chicken breast in water. When the chicken is cooked, place it aside to cool. Keep the water that the chicken has been cooking in. While waiting for the chicken to cool, chop your onions and garlic. Slice thinly your carrots and cabbage.

Shred chicken when it has cooled. In a large pan, add olive oil over medium heat. When oil is hot add garlic and onions, cook for 2 minutes. Add the carrots, celery and cabbage. When everything has cooked, add your canton noodles. Ladle in the water that the chicken has been cooking in. Stir to incorporate the veggies with the noodles. Add pepper and salt. Stir Constantly! Add one ladle of water at a time, until the noodles become soft.

Stuffed Zucchini with Turkey Sausage

Ingredients:

6 medium zucchini

3 tbsp. olive oil

1/2 cup chopped onion

1/2 cup mushrooms

1 tbsp. of white wine vinegar

1 1/2 diced tomatoes

1 cup of parmesan chees

1 egg, lightly beaten

2 tsp salt

2 tsp pepper

1 pound of ground turkey

Instructions:

Cut zucchini in half lengthwise. Scoop out insides, leaving shells about 1/4 inch thick.

Reserve about half of the insides.

Heat 2 Tbsp. of olive oil in a skillet on medium high heat.

Sauté` onion and garlic until soft and golden color. Add mushrooms and reserved Zucchini insides, and sauté` another 2 min.

In a separate skillet heat a Tbsp. of olive oil on medium high heat. Add the ground turkey. Lightly brown the brown turkey, stirring only occasionally.

After that stir in the onion ad mushroom mixture from the other pan. Add the vinegar. Stir in tomato, and cook 1 min. longer. Drain any excess fat. Remove mixture from heat and set aside.

When mixture has cooled, add 3/4th of the cheese, egg, salt and pepper. Fill zucchini shells with mixture. Fill a baking pan with 1/4 inch of water. Place filled zucchini halves in pan and bake at 375 degrees for 25 min., until lightly brown. Remove zucchini from pan and put the rest of the cheese on top and serve.

CHICKEN CRUST PIZZA

Ingredients:

16.0 oz. Ground Chicken - Extra Lean

1 cup, pieces or slices Mushrooms, fresh

1 cup Mozzarella finely shredded Part Skim cheese

1 cup Shredded Parmesan Cheese Natural Cheese

Black Olives – (can of sliced)

1/2 serving Sweet Mini Peppers 3, peppers about 5

1/2 cup Italian Stewed Tomatoes with Basil, Garlic, and Oregano

1 tbsp. Oregano, ground

3 clove Garlic

1 tbsp. Garlic powder

1 tbsp. Onion powder

1 tsp sugar substitute

Instructions:

Preheat oven to 450 degrees Line a baking sheet with parchment paper. Spray with cooking spray. In a bowl mix ground chicken, 1/2 of the Parmesan Cheese, and 1/2 of the Mozzarella, add 1/2 the seasoning. Oregano, Garlic powder, onion powder, salt, pepper and some Italian seasoning.

Place ground mixture onto cookie sheet and roll flat. Bake 12-15 minutes, until golden. While the crust is cooking make the pizza sauce. Blend 1 can of tomatoes, garlic cloves, and rest of seasonings. Smear cooked crust with Pizza sauce, add remaining cheese and toppings, and Bake until melted and bubbly 6-10 minutes. Serving Size: 1/8 of a Pizza

CHICKEN ADOBO

Ingredients

1 cup soy sauce

1 tsp Salt

1 tsp Pepper, black

1 cup cider Vinegar

Chicken Thigh, 1 unit (yield from 1 lb ready-to-cook)

1 clove Garlic

1 Onion, raw, 10 rings

3 dashes Pepper, black

5 tbsp. Canola Oil

Instructions:

Put the vegetable oil in a hot pan.

Slightly fry the chicken to remove its odor.

Put the chicken aside and add the garlic, onions, soy sauce, vinegar.

The combination of your sauce should suites your taste.

Put the chicken in again.

Then put the pepper and sugar. For the best taste, put a chili (sauce or raw)

Cover the pan and wait for 25-30 minutes until the chicken absorbed the sauce.

Ready to serve and eat.

BBQ Mango Chicken

Ingredients:

2 lbs of Chicken Breasts

6 to 8 tbsp. of BBQ sauce

4 oz. of Mango Puree

2/3 tbsp. Garlic Powder

Optional Dash of Bread Crumbs (for on top)

Instructions:

Preheat the oven for 375 degrees.

First mix the BBQ sauce, garlic powder, and puree mango (I use the magic bullet mixer)

Pour a third of the sauce into a baking dish.

Cut the chicken into 4 oz. pieces (8 servings) and place into baking dish. Cover with sauce (I always seem to have an ounce or so left over). Sprinkle bread crumbs if desired and place in the oven for 15 to 20 minutes, or until thoroughly cooked.

Enjoy with corn or baked beans to round out the meal

Healthy Chicken Sour Cream Enchilada's

Ingredients:

12oz. or about 3 chicken breasts

1cup chopped onion

Garlic powder to taste

Red pepper to taste

10 corn tortillas

½ cup cream of chicken soup

½ cup sour cream

1 cup fat free cheddar cheese

Cilantro

½ cup 1% milk

Instructions:

Boil chicken then shred into small pieces, sauté onion add to chicken season with garlic and pepper, Warm tortillas, Warm soup, sour cream and milk in sauce pan, fill tortillas with chicken, sprinkle a little cheese and cilantro in each one.

Pour sour cream sauce on top of all enchiladas and sprinkle with remaining cheese. Bake at 350 for 15 to 20 minutes.

Pancit with Miracle Noodles

Ingredients:

1 tbsp. Olive Oil

1/2 Bag of Coleslaw Mix

1/2 Onion, Thinly Sliced

1/2 Cup Snow Peas

2 Garlic Gloves, Minced

2 Boneless Chicken Thighs, Cooked and Chopped

1 Package of Miracle Noodles Angel Hair

1/2 Cup Chicken Broth

1tbsp. Soy or Tamari Sauce

1 tsp Ground Black Pepper

1 Lemon, Cut into Wedges

Instructions:

In a large wok or frying pan, sauté the cabbage and onions in olive oil over medium heat.

 Once all is nice and tender, add snow peas, garlic and cook until fragrant, 2-3min.

Add cooked chicken pieces, Miracle Noodles, broth, soy sauce, and ground black pepper.

Toss and bring to light boil, turn down heat and simmer for 5-10 minutes to allow all flavors to combine.

Place in serving bowls and squeeze lemon juice to taste.

Garlic Fried Cauliflower Rice

Ingredients:

1 head of cauliflower, chopped/grated into rice-like chunks

5 cloves of minced, fresh garlic (or more! if you love garlic)

1-2 eggs (depending on how much you like eggs)

1/2 tbsp of fish sauce (patis) - you can use salt to taste if you do not have fish sauce

2 tbsp olive oil

Garlic powder (optional)

Instructions:

Coat a non-stick skillet or wok with 1 tbsp. of olive oil and put on med-high heat

Once pan is hot, add the garlic and cook, stirring continuously, until every piece is brown - remove fromthe pan and set aside

Add another tbsp. of olive oil to pan and turn heat to high

Add grated cauliflower to pan and spread out so it covers the bottom of the pan, let cook for 1-2 minutes, depending on if you want it to be crispier. Stir all of the cauliflower and repeat until all of the cauliflower starts to turn more yellow/golden

Push all of the cauliflower to one side and crack the egg(s) into the empty space - let stand until edges start to brown and then scramble the eggs in the pan, breaking into small chunks and then mixing into the fried cauliflower

Drip the fish sauce throughout the mixture and continue to stir to ensure it spreads evenly

Plate the finished cauliflower fried rice and top with the browned garlic. Serve with chicken tocino and a fried egg or any other protein.

Filipino Style Pork Adobo

Ingredients;

4 gloves garlic

1 medium sized onion

1 tsp pepper

1 tsp peppercorns

1 tsp salt

3 laurel leaves

1/4 cup coconut aminoss

1/4 cup distilled white vinegar

1/4 cup sugar substitute

8 cups water

Instructions:

Cut pork belly into 2- inch cubes (your local butcher can do this)

Using a pot, sear pork belly cubes until the bottom of the pot is covered (don't stack pork cubes since it is important that both sides of your met is evenly seared. Do this until a good amount of fat comes out)

Remove meat for the pot

Sautee garlic and onion

Add pork and stir until golden brown

Add coconut aminos, salt, pepper, peppercorns and sweetener and stir

Add water and cover

Add Vinegar and laurel leaves after 4 -45 mins. Cook until meat is on the soft but still tender

Filipino skirt steak cauliflower fried Rice

Ingredients:

Simple cauliflower fried rice:

2 cups cauliflower rice

2-3 bulbs scallions chopped, separate white and green parts

2 small garlic cloves finely chopped

¼ tsp ginger grated

2 tsp coconut aminos

1 tsp sesame oil

Coarse salt to taste

Quick tomato sauce:

1 medium ripe tomato finely chopped

1 ½ tbsp. shallots finely chopped

2 tbsp. flat parsley finely chopped

Lime juice to taste

Instructions:

Prepare the steak: use a sharp knife to shallow slice/score the steak in a small criss-cross cut pattern to enable better marinating.* Marinate the steak overnight with ingredients under "steak seasonings" or at least 1-2 hours in the fridge.

Grill/pan-sear steak:

Add 1 tbsp. ghee to a well heated cast iron. Shake excess marinade from the steak and cook each side for 2-3 minutes per side for medium to medium-rare, depending on the thickness of the cut, basting the steak with ghee and steak juices. Set aside to rest.

Cauliflower rice:

Add 1 tbsp. ghee or avocado oil to a heated skillet, when hot lower the heat to medium, add white parts of chopped scallions and finely chopped garlic

Season with a small pinch of salt. Sauté until fragrant (about 10 seconds).

Add 2 cups cauli rice, grated ginger, coconut aminos, and sesame oil.

Season with a small pinch of salt. Stir fry quickly to cook the cauli rice to a soft (but not mushy) texture. Turn off the heat and stir-in green parts of scallion.

Serve: Slice steak against the grain. Serve it with cauliflower rice, fried egg, and top with tomato sauce.

CRISPY SISIG

Ingredients:

4 cups lechon kawali, chopped (deep fried port belly)

1 red bell pepper, seeded, cored and diced

1 medium onion, peeled and diced

5 Thai chili peppers, minced

1/2 cup calamansi juice

Salt and pepper to taste

Instructions:

In a large bowl, combine lechon kawali, bell pepper, onions, chili peppers and calamansi juice. Gently toss together to evenly distribute.

Season with salt and pepper to taste.

TURKEY APPLE WRAP

Ingredients:

1 Low carb, whole grain flat wrap *

3 Tbsp. Apple Butter

2 slices turkey breast deli meat

1/3 apple cored and thinly sliced

1 thin sliced provolone cheese

1/2 cup lettuce shredded

1 thin slice of onion

Instructions:

Spread the apple butter all over the flat wrap. Pile the rest of the ingredients on one half of the wrap and roll.

The best is to use a tart apple like a granny smith; however, you can use your favorite apple.

Lechón Pork

Ingredients:

5lb bone in pork shoulder (Boston butt)

1 grapefruit

1 orange

2 limes

1 lemon

4 garlic cloves

2 tbsp. salt

1 tbsp. oregano

1 tsp turmeric

1 tbsp. minced parsnip

1/3 cup diced cilantro, fresh

Instructions:

the pork needs to marinate for hours, preferably overnight.

Place pork in a large bowl.

In a large mortar with pestle (or food processor, although I rather like the ritual of grinding the mix by hand), mix & mash the garlic cloves, salt, oregano, turmeric, parsnip & cilantro with lemon & lime juice.

Once it's almost puree like in texture mix in the orange & grapefruit juice, This is your mojo!

Pour your mojo all over the pork & massage it well. It will be aromatic, juicy & soft.

Cover with plastic wrap & place in the fridge at least 8 hours, overnight or up to 24 hours. Turn it over twice, make the marinade in the afternoon At least an hour before you're ready to roast, set the pork out uncovered.

Pat the skin dry.

Place the pork shoulder on aluminum lined sheet pan, add the mojo to the sheet pan.

Cover with a loose aluminum tent.

Roast at 250F for at least 6 hours, up to 8 hours, until internal temperature reads 220F or fork tender.

Remove from oven. Bring oven to 450F.

Remove the aluminum tent & place uncovered roast in the oven for 15-20 minutes, until skin is golden & crispy.

Let is rest a few minutes before serving, but you can steal a piece of crispy skin, its tradition.

Remove the crispy skin and set aside

Using two forks, in a criss-cross motion, pull the pork meat apart

Pour any pan drippings on top

Cut up the skin and sprinkle over

Serve with cauli-rice, mashed yucca and salad

Bicol Express Recipe

Ingredients:

3 cups coconut milk

2 lbs pork belly, cut into strips

½ cup Shrimp Paste

1 tbsp. Garlic, minced

6 pieces Thai chili or Serrano pepper

3 tablespoons minced ginger

1 medium onion, minced

2 tbsp cooking oil

Salt and Pepper to taste

Instructions:

Heat a pan and then pour in the cooking oil.

Sauté the garlic, onion, and ginger

Add the pork and then continue cooking for 5 to 7 minutes or until the color becomes light   brown

Put in the shrimp paste and Thai chili or Serrano pepper. Stir.

Pour the coconut milk in. Bring to a boil. Simmer for 40 minutes or until the pork is tender

Add salt and ground black pepper to taste

Serve Hot. Enjoy!

CRISPY PATA RECIPE

Ingredients:

1 whole pig's leg (pata; about 3 to 4 lbs), cleaned

6 pieces dried bay leaves

2 tbsp. whole peppercorn

4 to 6 pieces star anise (optional)

6 tsp salt

2 tsp ground black pepper

2 to 3 tsps. garlic powder

12 to 15 cups water

8 to 12 cups cooking oil

Instructions:

Pour water in a cooking pot then let boil.

Put-in dried bay leaves, whole peppercorn, star anise, and 4 teaspoons of salt.

Add the whole pig's legs in the cooking pot then simmer until the leg becomes tender (about 45 to 60 minutes).

Remove the tender leg from the cooking pot and set aside until the temperature goes down.

Rub the leg with garlic powder, ground black pepper, and remaining salt. Let stand for 15 minutes to absorb the rub.

Heat a clean large cooking pot (preferably with cover) and pour-in cooking oil .When the oil becomes hot, deep fry the rubbed pork leg.

Continue cooking in medium heat until one side becomes crispy, and then cautiously flip the leg to crisp the other side. Note: Be extra careful in doing this procedure. Turn-off the heat; remove the crispy pork leg; and transfer it to a wide serving plate. Serve with soy sauce

Fish Fillet Ala Pobre with Tomato-Mango Salsa

Ingredients:

4 pieces fish fillet (tilapia, salmon, snapper)

1 head garlic, grind

1/4 cup butter

2 tbsp. soy sauce or Worcestershire sauce

Salt and pepper to taste

Canola oil for frying

Tomato-Mango Salsa:

4 pieces tomatoes (cut into small pieces)

1 medium-sized green mango(, cut into small pieces

1 onion, cut into small pieces

1/4 cup soy sauce or Worcestershire sauce

1/2 tsp ground pepper

1 tbsp. tomato sauce (optional)

1 green bell pepper, cut into small pieces(optional)

1 tbsp. chopped parsley (optional)

Instructions:

Season fish fillet with salt and pepper then fry until light brown.

Drain on paper towel then transfer to serving plate.

In a bowl, combine tomato-mango salsa ingredients then stir well. Set aside.

In a same pan, reduce oil then sauté garlic until light brown.

Add butter and soy sauce then stir until butter is melted.

Pour the sauce over fish fillet then serve with tomato-mango salsa.

Spicy Shrimp in Coconut Milk and Cilantro

Ingredients:

12 pieces jumbo shrimps, peeled and deveined

1 1/2 cup unsweetened coconut milk

2 large tomatoes, diced

1 red bell pepper, sliced thinly

4 cloves garlic, minced

1 tsp olive oil

1 tbsp. Lime juice

1/2 cup cilantro

2 pieces red chili chopped

Salt and pepper to taste

1 tsp chili sauce (optional)

Instructions:

In a pot, heat olive oil then sauté red bell pepper until soft.

Add garlic, cilantro, chili and tomatoes then continue sautéing for a minute.

Add coconut milk, chili sauce, salt and pepper then cover and simmer for 5 minutes in low heat.

Add shrimp and lime juice then cook for another 3 minutes.

Adjust seasoning according to taste and continue cooking until sauce is thicken.

Transfer to serving bowl and sprinkle with remaining cilantro. Serve and enjoy!

Spicy Fish Fillet with Tomatoes and Olives

Ingredients:

4 pieces fish fillet (tilapia, salmon, red snapper)

2 1/2 cups cherry tomatoes, halved

1 cup black olives, chopped

1/2 cup green bell pepper, diced(optional)

1 medium onion, chopped

2 cloves garlic, peeled and diced

2 tbsp. paprika

1/4 cup olive oil

Salt and pepper to taste

Instructions:

In a bowl, season fillets with paprika, salt and pepper.

In a frying pan, heat olive oil and fry fillet for 2 minutes.

In a saucepan, heat olive oil and sauté onion and garlic.

Add the tomatoes, bell pepper, chili flakes, salt and pepper then simmer for 3 minutes or until soft. Add a little water if necessary.

Place the fish fillets, cover and cook for another minutes.

Transfer salmon fillets to serving plate with the sauce.

Serve hot.

Ginisang Togue

Ingredients:

1/2 kilo sprouted mung beans (toge)

1/2 cup fried tofu diced

1/4 kilo pork, cut into small pieces

1 small-sized bell pepper, cut into strips

1 small-sized carrot, cut into strips

1/2 head garlic, chopped

1 medium-sized onion, chopped

1 medium-sized tomato, chopped

Fish sauce (patis) or salt and pepper to taste

Vegetable oil

Instructions:

In a frying pan, heat oil and fry pork until golden brown. Set aside.

Sauté garlic, onions and tomatoes.

Add fried tofu and pork then a little water and pork broth cubes. Cook for 1 minute.

Adjust seasoning with salt and pepper.

Add sprouted mung beans, carrots and bell pepper and cook for 5 minutes or until vegetables are half-cooked.

Remove from heat. Serve with steamed rice.

You may also add shrimp and green beans

Filipino-Style Steamed Snapper Recipe

Ingredients:

1 (3/4 kilo)whole snapper, scaled, gutted

1 thumb-sized ginger, shredded

4 green onions, thinly sliced diagonally

1 piece red chili, deseeded and sliced thinly

1 1/2 tbsp. soy sauce

1/2 tsp oil (olive, sesame)

1 tsp sugar substitute

Fresh coriander leaves, chopped (optional)

Instructions:

In a bowl, combine green onion, ginger, red chili, soy sauce, sesame oil and sugar.

Place the fish on large heatproof plate. Pour the mixtures evenly over the fish. Marinate for 15-30

 minutes..

In a wok, add enough water for about 5cm depth. Place the steaming rack over the wok.

Place the plate with marinade fish on steaming rack.

Bring to boil over medium heat. Steam for 15 minutes or until fish is done.

Remove the plate from the wok and

Serve and enjoy

Fish Fillet Curry

Ingredients:

1/2 kilo fish fillets (tuna, salmon, lapu-lapu, tanigue)

2 tbsp. curry powder

1 cup unsweetened coconut milk

1 onion, chopped

3 cloves garlic, minced

1 thumb-sized ginger, minced

1 tbsp fresh lime or calamansi juice

2 potatoes cut into cubes

2 carrots cut into cubes

2 pieces green and red bell peppers, cut into cubes

2 tbsp. olive oil

Salt and pepper to taste

tbsp. Cornstarch (optional)

1/2 red chili, sliced diagonally (optional)

Instructions:

In a bowl, marinate fish with lime juice, pepper and salt for 30 minutes.

In a separate bowl, combine curry powder, coconut milk and cornstarch. Mix until dissolved.

In a pan, heat oil then fry potatoes and carrots until light brown. Drain and set aside.

In a pan, heat oil and sauté ginger, garlic and onions.

Add the curry mixtures then stir and bring to boil.

Add fish then simmer in a low heat for 10 minutes or tender. (Do not stir but prevent fish from
 Sticking.)

Add bell peppers, potatoes and carrots then season with salt and pepper according to taste.

Simmer for another 2 minutes.

Transfer the fish into serving plate with sauce on top. Serve hot with steamed rice.

Made in the USA
Coppell, TX
15 February 2025

45975132R00023